CRIMSOC REPORT 6:

Torture in Police Custody in Bangladesh:

An Exploration of Human Rights Violations

Published by CRIMSOC 2016

Los Angeles, United States

CONTENTS

Page 3: CRIMSOC Editor's Introduction

Page 6: Abstract

Page 7: Introduction

Page 10: Results and Analysis

Page 17: Tables

Page 21: Content Analysis

Page 36: Conclusion

Page 39: References

Torture in Police Custody in Bangladesh: An Exploration of Human Rights Violations

*Mohammad Ashraful Alam[1] and Mahmuda Akter[2]

1. Associate Professor

Department of Criminology & Police Science,

Mawlana Bhashani Science & Technology University, Tangail-1902, Bangladesh.

Founding Member: Human Trafficking Global Organization, USA.

Member: World Society of Victimology (WSV),

Treasurer: Bangladesh Society of Criminology,

*Corresponding Author: Contact: Cell: +8801733173548

Email: maalam.cps@gmail.com, prodip_sust2005@yahoo.com

2. MS Student

Department of Criminology & Police Science,

Mawlana Bhashani Science & Technology University, Tangail-1902, Bangladesh.

Former Intern: Transparency International Bangladesh (TIB),

Former Intern: Bangladesh Legal Aid & Services Trust (BLAST),

Contact: Cell: +8801557172372

E-mail: mahmudaakterhappy72@gmail.com, mahmudaakter.happy@yahoo.com

CRIMSOC EDITOR'S INTRODUCTION

Liam James Leonard PhD, Senior Editor of CRIMSOC Department of Sociology, California State University, Los Angeles, United States

As the Founding Editor of CRIMSOC, I have always believed in supporting research from all parts of the globe. For this reason, I am very pleased to introduce this most significant piece of research, which examines the problem of human rights violation and torture in custodial settings in Bangladesh.

This is the first published research into this form of human rights violations in Bangladesh, and as such represents a breakthrough for its authors and for criminology in Asia. As someone who has taught and promoted human rights within the prison system in Ireland, I have an understanding of the unique problems such research represents. For that reason, we at CRIMSOC invite the wider criminology world to support this research and hopefully there will be further studies of this kind across the different nations of the world. As the great South African leader Nelson Mandela once said:

> *"It is said that no one truly knows a nation until one has been inside its jails. A nation should not be judged by how it treats its highest citizens, but its lowest ones."*

With this in mind, we must congratulate the authors of this insightful work. I look forward to future research from them, and to continuing CRIMSOC's record of significant publications in relevant areas of criminology and penology.

Abstract

Torture has become synonymous with the law-enforcement agency which affects the credibility of rule of law in Bangladesh. The major aim of this study was to explore the nature of torture in police custody from victim perspectives in Bangladesh. The additional aims were to analyze the causes and consequences of torture in police custody and find out the drawbacks to prevent torture victimization. This study was based on the triangulation of case study, content analysis and key informant interview through integration of both quantitative and qualitative manner. From this study, custodial torture occurred for structural deficiencies in justice system where middle class accused (31%) are prone to victimization at trail stage; arrested by polices without warrant (75%); tortured both physically and psychologically (63%) to obtaining confession and bribery (50%); which results serious physical, psychological, and social-economic problem (69%) to victim.

Keywords: Custodial Violence, Torture, Police Custody, Confession, Custodial Victimization.

1. Introduction

Torture in police custody has existed for a long time in Bangladesh. This becomes problem is greater than any other form of violence because victims of such violence are unable to protest against it. Besides, the country's civil society, media, and scholars largely agree with the police view that torture is necessary for criminal investigations. No direct evidence is available to substantiate the charge of torture or causing hurt resulting into death or other injury, as the police lockup where generally torture is caused is away from public gaze and the witnesses are either policemen or co-prisoners who are highly reluctant to appear as prosecution witness due to fear of retaliation by the superior officers of the police (Hadi, 2012). In spite of the constitutional and statutory provisions contained in the national constitution, criminal procedure code and the penal code, the Torture and Custodial Death (Prevention) Act, (2013), various UN convention on custodial torture and UDHR (1948), International Covenant on Civil and Political Rights (ICCPR) etc. aimed at safeguarding personal liberty and life of a citizen, the increasing incidence of torture and deaths in police custody has been alarming. Consequently, the levels of impunity have reached new heights and there is also a new pattern of torture in Bangladesh, it lamented.

During 2004- 2015(April) in total 394 accused (alive 231, dead 163) were allegedly tortured by police (ASK, 2014). For the period of the first six months of 2015, three persons were allegedly tortured to death by the police where two persons were reported beaten to death; one was beaten to death by the police, 30 persons were shot in the leg by the law enforcement agencies after arrest (ODHIKAR, 2015). Besides, 10 persons were allegedly tortured to death by the police in

2014 and in 2013 while 5 persons were dead in 2012, 14 persons were dead in 2011 whereas 20 persons were dead in 2010 (ODHIKAR, 2014).

Even though there is no definition of 'torture' in the penal laws; acts amounting to torture in police custody are common and almost become systematic in Bangladesh. Torture and other ill-treatment were widespread and committed with impunity (Rafiqul & Solaiman, 2004). The High Court bench delivered the verdict on the writ petition issuing a 15-point directive on the government to be followed by the law enforcement agencies in arresting, detaining, remanding and treating suspects on April 7, 2003 (Halim, 2009). The decision came in the case of the Bangladesh Legal Aid and Services Trust (BLAST) and Others Vs. Bangladesh and Others, where several human rights and legal aid, non-government organizations filed a writ petition in the High Court challenging the abuse of police powers to arrest without warrant under Section 54 of the Code of Criminal Procedure, 1898 and the abuse of powers regarding taking the accused into remand or police custody under section 167 of the Code of Criminal Procedure (55 DLR, 2003). To date, no such glass partitioned rooms have yet been constructed and torture and other degrading forms of treatment are still meted out to an accused in remand (Khan, 2003). But, those directions of court are not followed properly in practice and the number of victim of torture in police custody is increasing.

The majority of torture survivors suffer from the consequences of repressive cycles of torture by law-enforcing agents for generations. They drift in emptiness in all aspects of their life. The survivors' mental and physical capabilities are damaged in a way that negatively affects their personal, socio familial and economic life (Munir, 1998). On the other side, the political, bureaucratic and criminal justice systems complement each other to patronize and solidify torture and deny justice to the deserving. Many survivors see torture as the key pillar of the state, contradicting theoretical definition of state from political science perspective (AHRC, 2013).

This paper has been prepared to focus on the issues of nature and extent of torture in police custody in Bangladesh. Besides, this paper included the analysis of the causes and consequences of torture in police custody to the victim. In addition, to find out the drawbacks to bring to an end of torture victimization in police custody has also analyzed here.

2. Objectives

The principal aim of this study was to explore the nature of torture in police custody from victim perspectives in Bangladesh. The additional purposes of this study were:

i. To investigate the causes of torture victimization in police custody;
ii. To identify how the weak legal and institutional mechanisms making guilty of police for denial of justice;
iii. To understand the consequences of torture in police custody to the victim; and
iv. To find out the drawbacks to prevent torture victimization in police custody.

3. Methodology

Descriptive type research design has used to conduct this research. This study was based on triangulation of case study, content analysis, and key informant interview through the integration of both quantitative and qualitative manner. Case study has conducted through in depth interview from individual victimized person in police custody in Dhaka city, Bangladesh. Total 17 case studies of custodial torture in police custody were selected within the Dhaka city from the records of two national famous non-government organization named Ain O Salish Kendra (ASK) and ODHIKAR. Purposive sampling method was used to conduct the case study from victim of torture in police custody. In addition, for conducting content analysis, data has been collected from two famous Bengali newspapers, The Daily Prothom Alo and The Daily Jugantor; and the most circulated English newspaper The Daily Star; and the famous online newspaper Dhaka Tribune from January, 2015 to April, 2015 through a self-completion checklist. And, Key Informant Interview has taken through in depth interview method from the 5 experts including lawyers, teachers and experienced professional researcher related to this field. Most importantly, thematic analysis was used for both Case study and KII analysis. The content analyses were processed through examining newspapers with particular checklist, coding, categorization and tabulation. The Statistical Program for Social Science (SPSS), Microsoft Office Word and Excel is used for data analyzing and interpretation. Besides, data were also analyzed through various univariate and bivariate analysis ((table and graph) to correlate the variable which includes the frequency, cross-tabulation and test of hypothesis by chi-square distribution.

4. Results and Analysis

4.1 Thematic Analysis of the Case Study

4.1.1 Socio-demographic Characteristics of the Respondents

The case study reveals that they were youth people aged between 24-35 years (all seventeen respondents including fifteen male and two female). These case study shows and majority of them are from Islamic religious background (fifteen respondents) than Hindu (two respondents). Majority of the respondents (12) were unmarried while few respondents are married (7) tortured in police custody. Besides, majority of the respondents' educational education level are graduation (six respondents) and most of them are private service holder (four respondents), journalist and politics (three respondents). From this study, it has become evident that poor (six respondents) and middle class (eleven respondents) are prone to victimization in the custody of police.

4.1.2 Torture has Become Common in Police Custody for All Types of Crime

The practice of torture in police custody has become a potential scene in Bangladesh, particularly in Dhaka city. According to this study, 6 respondents victim of torture were arrested under the offence of political crime and individually 3 respondent victim of torture were arrested under theft and robbery. Besides, independently 2 respondent victim of torture were arrested under explosion, arson and murder while separately 1 respondent victim of torture were arrested under religious terrorism, child trafficking, drug trafficking and illegal prostitution. That means, the risk of torture in the custody for accused has turned into very regular in Bangladesh.

Torture is widely practiced by the police against individuals most of the time, individuals who are suspects in crimes because several local NGOs in Indonesia have conducted research on this and they concluded that the police subject around 70-80% of suspects to torture and ill treatment in Indonesia (Rana, 2013).

Moreover, torture is widespread and it is believed to be an efficient crime investigation strategy in Nepal. Torture is widespread because there is no effective law or mechanism and resources insufficient to undertake criminal investigations (Rafiqul & Solaiman, 2004). Besides, in Cambodia, torture is commonly used during police questioning. The policing system is very primitive and no modernization has taken place there which decrease the human right and dignity in a large number (Human rights watch, 2013).

4.1.3 Arbitrary Torture is Applying in Police Custody in the Name of Investigation

It has turn out to be a general issue that the number of arrest and torture in the custody increases during unstable political condition in Bangladesh. Accordingly, from 2011-2015 this study shows, 4 respondents the victim faces the torture in police custody from the year of 2015, 3 respondents in 2014, 4 respondents in 2013, 5 respondents in 2012, 1 respondent in 2011. This study also shows, 5 respondent victims were arrested without warrant while 12 respondent victims were arrested with warrant in Dhaka city. The use of section 54 of CrPC still remains questionable whether they are following the rule of high court (Sikdar, 2000).

In addition, this study shows, the victims were detained from one day to more than two months (all seventeen cases) and also sentenced for specific time (four cases). Although the provisions of confining an accused in the custody are laid down in section 167 of the *CrPC* state that, the stage of investigation would not be more than 15 days in a whole in police custody or jail custody and when the investigation cannot be completed within 120 days from the date of receipt of the information relating to the commission of the offence (Rahman, 2009).

In India and Cambodia, torture is commonly used during police interrogations and even police officers are trained and allowed to use force, including torture (AI, 2008). Moreover, torture is the de facto standard procedure of the police and the military in Philippines. In every arrest, interrogation, and detention, torture is applied in varying degrees, either physical or psychological torture (AI, 2014).

4.1.4 Accused Criminal Become Victim of Torture in Each Stage of Justice

According to this study, 7 victims of police torture were tortured that started from their home and 7 victims of police torture were tortured that started from public place and police station. Besides, 11 respondent's faces torture in the police custody at the trail stage while other 6 respondent become torture victim at the arrest and pre trail procedure of justice in Dhaka city. So, the police officers are violating their behavioral conducting rules and the issue of fair justice is on the question of impunity in Bangladesh.

In India, corruption and the proceeds of corruption form the denominators are forged in the justice (Aziz, 2010). Their ruling environment expects the law enforcement agencies to remain corrupt, to be brutal to the ordinary citizen and to enforce all forms of state writ upon the people. This leaves a narrow common space for politically questioning state actions in practicing custodial torture (AHRC, 2013).

The government connives to maintain a bad policing system as it benefits most politicians in the Srilanka. There is no will at all to implement the law against torture. Consequently, the police is using torture in the pre-trail and trail stage at high rate (Bamford & Sarre, 2000). Investigations into allegations of torture have been stopped. There is no implementation of the recommendations of the CAT Committee or UN agencies (Basoglu, 2013).

4.1.5 Torture to Attain Confession and as a Means of Early Solution of Case

Torture is police custody is used as a technique of early solution of case. According to this study in Dhaka city, 6 respondent were tortured by police to obtaining confession, 9 respondent were tortured by police both confession and bribery and 1 respondent were tortured by police for organization power or political order within four months of this year.

In Thailand, torture is widely used by the police, army, and other state security forces as a tool of repression and routine form of punishment. Throughout the country, police torture suspects during interrogation and/or to obtain a confession (Catani, 2013). In the nine years since martial law and the emergency decree have been in force in southern Thailand, citizen's report that people who complain about torture and arbitrary detention are intimidated and punished. Rather than fighting terror, the state security forces have also become agents of it (Islam, 2007).

In addition, murderer police officers often enjoy celebrity status by being referred as encounter specialists in India, even promoted so by the media (Jeevan, 2001). These encounter specialists are those who shoot to kill persons whom they suspect to be criminals if deny to confess at charge. It is natural, that in a country where torture is actively condoned and expected to be the defining character of all law enforcement agencies, the law enforcement agencies use this possibility of generating fear upon the people as a means for encounter (Human rights watch, 2008).

4.1.6 Torture in Custody the is Cruel Forms Police Corruption (Bribery)

Bribery or greed for money is the most hateful reason for custodial torture and one that seems to be on the increase. According to this study, 9 respondent victims are tortured in the custody for the demand of bribery. At the level of police station, a number of Policeman use brutality to extract money from suspects and innocent persons. The legal situation and the nature of evidence facilitate the process and giving what he does an air of finality, which gives him the unintended power to extract money and escape the corrective process of supervision.

In Pakistan and Sri Lanka, while investigating a case, police threaten to, practicing physical and mental torture until accused gives money (AHRC, 2013).Torture and bribery are carried out by police personnel are always connected in Mianmar. The basic problem is that the police are not paid enough for example; many get approximately 40 USD, per month and there is no mechanism to control corruption and extortion in Combodia (AI, 2014). As well, in Indonesia, police do not formally arrest him/her for some days and ask for bribes to file cases in which bail is possible and, if the bribe is not paid, then the person is arrested under a heinous crime as the punishment for not bribing the police (Hadi, 2012).

4.1.7 Practice of Physical Torture Causes Severe Physical Harm to Victim

According to this study, physical torture was common for all 17 respondent victims. The general types of physical torture were confined in dark cell; beating, kicked and slapped; hot water treatment; electric shock; cracking nails; urinated over, inadequate food and water; rolling from ring etc. Beating is today the most common method that involved kicking and punching and also the use of sticks, gun-butts etc. Allegations of victims having needles pushed under their fingernails, being burnt with cigarettes and urinated over. So, the victims of torture in the police custody are seriously physically abused in Bangladesh.

After the torture in custody, victims were suffered a range of physical effects including insomnia, appetite disturbance, lethargy, headaches, muscle tension, nausea, and decreased. It is common for these reactions to persist for some time after the crime has occurred. Some victims were experience long-term side effects as a result of the crime committed against them (Malik, 2007).

4.1.8 Life Turned Into Imbalanced for Victims of Psychological Torture in Custody

According to this study, psychological torture was also common for all 17 respondent victims' like- use of slang words; threat of killing/disappearance; threat of lodging false case, threat of sexual harassment and threat of harassment of family etc. As torture is usually experienced as more serious than a crime, an accident or misfortune, it is difficult to come to terms with the fact that loss and injury have been caused by the deliberate act of another human being.

From this study, common reactions to custodial torture were split into four stages- the initial reaction included shock, fear, anger, helplessness, disbelief and guilt. Some of these reactions reoccur at a later stage as well. A period of disorganization followed these initial reactions. Life seemed to slow down and become meaningless. Previously held beliefs and faiths no longer provide comfort. Behavioral responses might include increased alcohol or substance abuse, fragmentation of social relationships, avoidance of people and situations associated with the crime, and social withdrawal.

Table No 1: Comparative Case Study of the Victim of Police Torture in Custody

	Case Study-1	Case Study-2	Case Study-3	Case Study-4	Case Study-5	Case Study-6
Age	32	25	24	29	34	35
Occupation	Business	Truck Driver	Student	Day laborer	Tailor	Private service
Sex	Male	Male	Male	Male	Female	Male
Education level	H.S.C	Primary	Graduate	S.S.C	Primary	Graduate
Marital Status	Unmarried	Unmarried	Unmarried	Married	Married	Unmarried
Religion	Islam	Islam	Hindu	Islam	Islam	Islam
Economic Status	Middle	Poor	Poor	Middle	Poor	Middle
Year of torture	2012	2011	2015	2012	2013	2012
Crime of arrest	Political riot	Theft	Arson	Theft	Child trafficking	Murder
Place of Torture	Own home and police station	Police station	Police station	Police Station	Police Station	Public place and Police Station
Stage of Torture	Arrest and trail	Pre-trail and trail	Trail	Trail	Pre-trail and trail	Trail
Reason of Torture	Obtain confession.	Gain confession and bribery.	Gain confession and bribery.	Obtain confession; and recover property and bribery.	Obtain confession.	Gain confession and bribery.
Types of Torture	Beating with rod and batons; kicked; tied with rope; threat of more severe torture.	Beating; squatting naked, humiliation; urinate pressure; confined in dark cell, demand huge bribery.	Hot water treatment; Beating; cracking finger nails with pliers; threat of killing; and demand bribery.	Hanging from the ceiling; beating; stripped naked and threat of bribery.	Beating with bamboo whips and batons; used slang words; shooting her sons's leg and threat of sexual abuse.	Beating in hands and legs; urinated over; inadequate food and threat of false case.
Current status of case	Detained for three months and in bail at present.	Detained for 25 days and in bail at present.	Detained for fifteen days and released.	Detained for more than one month, pay compensation and bribe and released.	Sentenced for three months.	Sentenced for two years.

Outcome of Torture	Trouble in hearing; finger damaged; confidence decreases; and economic loss.	Severe back pain; sleep deprivation and mental imbalance.	Heart and kidney problem; cannot bear any stress, economic loss for paying bribery.	Pain in arms, legs, chest; economic loss for paying bribery.	Pain in both hands and neck; shout unnecessarily, mentally disturbed.	Sleep deprivation; economic loss; family reputation decreases and narrow mental condition.

Table No 1: Comparative Case Study of the Victim of Police Torture in Custody (Continue)

	Case Study-7	Case Study-8	Case Study-9	Case Study-10	Case Study-11	Case Study-12
Age	28	27	24	31	29	26
Occupation	Garment worker	Business	Teacher	Business	Private service	Student
Sex	Male	Male	Male	Male	Male	Male
Education level	S.S.C	H.S.C	Graduate	Graduate	H.S.C	Graduate
Marital Status	Unmarried	Unmarried	Unmarried	Unmarried	Unmarried	Unmarried
Religion	Islam	Islam	Islam	Islam	Islam	Islam
Economic Status	Poor	Middle	Middle	Middle	Middle	Middle
Year of torture	2013	2014	2013	2014	2013	2012
Crime of arrest	Drug Trafficking	Political hartal	Religious Terrorism	Robbery	Political Assault	Murder
Place of Torture	Police station	Public place and police station	Public place and police station	Police Station	Police Station	Public place and Police Station
Stage of Torture	Arrest and trail	Pre-trail and trail	Trail	Pre-trail and trail	Pre-trail	Trail
Reason of Torture	Obtain confession.	Gain confession and bribery.	Gain confession and bribery.	Obtain confession; recover property and bribery.	Obtain confession and demand bribery.	Gain confession and bribery.

Types of Torture	Confined in dark cell, beating with rod; inadequate food; burn with cigarette; threat of false case.	Confined in dark cell; hot water treatment; beat with metallic rod and demand huge bribery.	Beating with bamboo whips; pressed with rod; threat of false case demand bribery.	Beaten by stick and rod; rolling; electric shock; red chili powder spread; demand bribery.	Beating with batons; used slang words; slapped.	Beating in legs with sticks; rolling by ring and demand bribery.
Current status of case	Detained for four days and now in bail.	Detained for nine days and in bail at present.	Detained for fourteen days and now in bail.	Detained for six days and now in bail.	Detained for ten days and now in bail.	Detained for one month and in bail at present.
Outcome of Torture	Trouble in arms ached; finger burned; mental confidence decreases.	Left paralyzed from the waist down; sleep deprivation and mental fear.	Heart problem; become unconscious; shouts without any reasons and economic loss.	Failure to move chest and neck; sleep deprivation; frustration and family reputation decreases..	Pain in both legs and fail to walk; mentally disturbed and economic loss.	Pain in both legs and fail to move; misbehave with all and economic loss.

Table No 1: Comparative Case Study of the Victim of Police Torture in Custody (Continue)

	Case Study-13	Case Study-14	Case Study-15	Case Study-16	Case Study-17
Age	32	30	35	29	24
Occupation	Journalist	Private service	Politician	Garment worker	Private service
Sex	Male	Male	Male	Female	Male
Education level	Post graduation	H.S.C	Graduate	S.S.C	Primary
Marital Status	Married	Unmarried	Married	Married	Unmarried
Religion	Islam	Islam	Islam	Islam	Islam
Economic Status	Middle	Middle	Middle	Poor	Poor
Year of torture	2014	2015	2012	2015	2015
Crime of arrest	Reasonable Suspicion	Explosion	Political Assault and drug	Illegal prostitution	Political

			dealing		Hartal picketing
Place of Torture	Public place and police station	Public place and police station	Home and police station	Home and police station	Public place and police station
Stage of Torture	Pre-trail	Pre-trail and trail	Pre-trail and trail	Trail	Pre-trail and trail
Reason of Torture	Organizational power	Gain confession and bribery.	Gain confession.	Obtain confession.	Obtain confession.
Types of Torture	Beating with stick; inadequate water; and threat of disappearance.	Beat with rod; electric shock, urinated over, demand huge bribery and threat of crossfire.	Beating by rolling; kicked with boot; hot water method.	Beaten and rolling; verbal abuse, unusual physical contact; inadequate food and threat of rape.	Rolled by heavy wooden roller; crushed muscles; kicking on stomach.
Current status of case	Detained for one day.	Detained for two months and in bail at present.	Detained for five days and now in bail.	Sentenced of two month imprisonment.	Sentenced of six month imprisonment.
Outcome of Torture	Severe pain in head and frustrated on the rule of law.	Severe pain in legs and chest; sleep deprivation; failure to trust on other and economic loss.	Broke of bone; breathing problems and damage lungs and mental disturbance.	Acute pain in the chest and neck, sleep deprivation; fear and frustration and family reputation decreases.	Pain in muscles and stomach; impairment of eye and hearing problem and self blaming.

According to Table 1, the present study shows the victims of torture were youth people aged between 24-35 years (including fifteen male and two female respondents). Most of them are from Islamic religious background (fifteen respondents) than Hindu (two respondents). Majority of their education level is graduate level (six respondents) while others education level is primary (three respondents), secondary (three respondents), higher secondary (three respondents) and post graduation level (two respondents). Most of the respondent victim's professions are business (three respondents) and journalism (three respondents) while political leaders (one respondent), private service holder (four respondents), teacher (one respondent), student, (two respondents), garment worker (two respondents), separately single respondent are tailor, truck driver and day labor also become torture victim in custody. Moreover, poor (six respondents) and middle class (eleven respondents) people are prone to victimization in the custody of police.

Table 1 also shows, five respondents victim were arrested without warrant while in twelve arrested with warrant from the year of 2011- 2015. According to this study, majority of the victim of torture were arrested under the offence of political crime (six respondents) while others were arrested for drug trafficking (one respondent), murder (two respondents), explosion and arson (two respondents), religious terrorism (one respondent), theft and robbery (three respondents), child trafficking (one respondent) and illegal prostitution (one respondent). In addition, this study shows most of the victim from the public place to police station and detained for a long time at trail stage. Moreover, victim faced police torture in the home (three respondents), public place (seven respondents) and police station.

According to Table 1, the reason of torture is not only obtaining confession (six respondents), but to attain both confession and bribery (nine respondents) and for organization power or political order (one respondent). Also, this study shows, the victims were detained from one day to more than two months and sentenced for specific period (four respondents). Besides, all respondents become the victim of physical torture includes confined in dark cell; beating, kicked and slapped; hot water treatment; electric shock; cracking nails; urinated over, inadequate food and water; rolling from ring etc. Besides, the psychological torture towards victim includes use of slang words; threat of killing/disappearance; threat of lodging false case, sexual harassment and harassment of family etc.

4.2 Content Analysis of the Study

4.2.1 Presentation of the News of Torture in Police Custody in the Newspapers

Newspaper plays an important role in representing the law and order in contemporary societies. According to Table-2, during January-April, 2015 the most number of news of torture in police custody is published by The Daily Nayadiganta (37.5 percent). After that, the Daily Dhaka Tribune (Online) (25 percent) also published a good number of torture news in police custody. Besides, Daily Prothom Alo (18.8 percent) and Daily Star (18.8 percent) published equal news of torture in police custody is published during January-April, 2015.

Not all crime victims receive equal attention in the newspaper. According to Table-2, the most number of incident of torture in police custody occurred in the month of February (37.5 percent) as the political situation become violent on the issue of 10th parliament election between government and opposite party in 2015. Besides, during the month of January (31.3 percent) the incident of torture in police custody were also high. But the incident of torture in police custody gradually decreases during March (18.8 percent) and April (12.5 percent) than the previous two months.

Table 2: Presentation Torture News in Police Custody in the Newspapers

Presentation Torture News in Police Custody		Number	Percent (%)
Newspapers Names	The Daily Prothom Alo	3	18.8 %
	The Daily Nayadiganta	6	37.5 %
	The Daily Star	3	18.8 %
	The Daily Dhaka Tribune	4	25.0 %
	Total	16	100 %
Month of Incident of Torture	January	5	31 %
	February	6	37 %
	March	3	19 %
	April	2	13 %
	Total	16	100 %

4.2.2 Socio Demographic Characteristics of Victim (Secondary study)

From Table-3, this study expose that young adult people are becoming more victimized of police torture in custody that belongs to the age group of 26 to 35 years (56.3 percent). Besides, the people belonging to the group of 36 to 45 years (18.8 percent) and the group of 16 to 25 years (12.5 percent) also faces the police torture in custody, Moreover, few child and middle aged young people are becoming victimized of police torture in custody that belongs to the age group of below 15 years (6.3 percent) and the group of up to 45 years (6.3 percent). So, in the study, maximum young people of 26-35 aged groups who are becoming more victimized of police torture in custody.

From the study, Table-3 shows the distribution of tortured victim in police custody on their sex where male (93.8 percent) are higher than female (6.3 percent). This distribution reflects that the highest numbers of male who become victim of police torture in custody are published more in the newspapers.

Education is directly related to the socio-economic condition of individual. According to Table-3, 3.3 percent of the victims education level are primary, 12.5 percent of the victims belong to the educational qualification of S.S.C, 43.8 percent of the victims belong to the educational qualification of the H.S.C. and 25 percent of the victims belong to the educational qualification of the Undergraduate level and 12.5 percent of the victims belong to the educational qualification of up to Graduate. So, in this study, majority of victim's education level is up to higher secondary level although all levels of educational back ground are represented in the study.

Occupation plays an important role in ascertaining the dignity of the individual in the society. According to this study, Table-3 shows, 18.8 percent of the victims of police torture in custody are student, 12.5 percent of the victims are service holder, 25 percent of the victims are businessman, 6.3 percent of the victims are journalist and 37.5 percent of the victims are actively involved in politics. So, in this study, majority of victims are from the political background who are arrested by polices for several reasons based on political issues and become illegal police torture in the custody.

Table 3: Socio Demographic Characteristics of Victim

Socio Demographic Characteristics		Number	Percent (%)
Age group	Below 15	1	6.3 %
	16-25	2	12.5 %
	26-35	9	56.3 %
	36-45	3	18.8 %
	45+	1	6.3 %
	Below 15	1	6.3 %
	Total	16	100 %
Sex	Male	15	93.8 %
	Female	1	6.3%
	Total	16	100 %
Level of Education	Primary	1	6.3 %
	SSC	2	13 %
	HSC	7	44 %
	Under Graduate	4	25.0 %
	Graduate+	2	12.5 %
	Total	120	100.0%
Occupation	Student	3	18.8 %
	Service	2	12.5 %
	Business	4	25.0 %
	Journalism	1	6.3 %
	Politics	6	37.5 %
	Total	120	100.0%

4.2.3 Nature of Torture Victimization in Police Custody

The weakness of general laws in Bangladesh produces the scope of violating the laws rather than preserving. Table-4 shows, only 25 percent of the victims of police torture in custody were arrested by police with warrant while 75 percent of the victims were arrested without warrant. So, majority of victims are arrested by polices without warrant under section 54 for several reasons based specially political issues and tortured more in the custody to in misusing section 164 and 167 of the code of criminal procedure during January to April, 2015. According to

AHRC (2013), unfortunately, in absence of any proper guideline, Magistrates and Judges of Bangladesh creates sufficient room for the police, who are arbitrary by practice and training, to abuse power as there has been no mechanism established to hold the police accountable.

According to Table-4, 25 percent of the victims of police torture in custody were accused for petty crime while 56.30 percent were accused for political crime. Besides, 12.5 percent of the victims were accused for murder and 6.3 percent were accused for illegal gambling. So, in this study, majority of victims were accused political crime due to unstable political situation that are arrested in a high number and tortured in the police custody. Consequently, many innocent people are arrested by police and become victim of torture in police custody.

In this study, Table-4 shows, 68.8 percent of the victims of police torture in custody were accused for first time while 6.3 percent were accused for second times and 25 percent of the victims were accused for many times. So, in this study, majority of victims were accused for first time who not regular criminal in nature and become illicit police torture in the custody. Our justice system and society are labeling them as criminals and torture in the police custody leads them to an uncertain life. An overworked, under-resourced, badly paid police force is resort to torture and degrading treatment in order to hasten their investigation (Rana, 2013).

Besides, Table-4 shows, 75 percent of the victims were tortured in the police custody during arrest and pre trail while 12.5 percent were tortured during trail and 12.5 percent of the victims were tortured sentencing. So, in this study, the newspaper represents that the majority of victims were tortured during arrest and pre-trail stage in the name of remand to obtain information of crime incident. Reality goes unrecorded to such an extent that nobody can provide credible statistics about the number of remand granted every day in Bangladesh, legally and illegally is a matter calling for special attention, of the human rights groups (AHRC, 2013).

From this study, Table- 4 shows, 50 percent of the victims were tortured in the police custody to obtain confession of commission of criminal; offence while 37.5 percent were tortured to receive bribery from accused and 12.5 percent of the victims were tortured for political or organization power of authority. So, the newspaper represents that the majority of victims were tortured to obtain information of crime incident and economic benefit of police. According to Malik (2007), lack of profound training in this regard is also a tremendous problem. Sometimes pressure from vested groups indirectly accelerates the whole process. Colonial degenerated mentality, traditional oppressive mindset, lack of right based approach, soaring ignorance about constitutional rights and human rights are also major problems.

From this study, Table-4 shows, 62.5 percent of the victims were physically tortured in the police custody while 12.5 percent were psychologically tortured. Moreover, 25 percent of the victims were both physically and psychologically tortured. So, in this study, the newspaper represents that the majority of victims were tortured both physically and psychologically which have a long term pessimistic effect on victim's personal and socio-economic life. According to Rafiqul and Solaiman (2004), police are poorly trained about the dangers of interrogation and false confession. Police officers are rarely instructed regarding how to avoid torturous mechanism of eliciting confessions, how to understand what causes false confessions, or how to recognize the forms false confessions take or their distinguishing characteristics.

Torture victim in police custody often leads to lasting intellectual and substantial health problems. According to this study, Table-4 illustrates, 68.8 percent of the victims were physically injured in the police custody while 18.8 percent were psychologically harmed. Moreover, 12.5 percent of the victims were dead due to police torture in custody. So, in this study, the newspaper represents that the majority of victims were tortured which results physically injury and the matter of mental harm and death is a major problem in our society. Berliner, Nikkelsen and Bovbjerg (2004) states that, to fatigue and frustration of victims extended with the economic problem, living below poverty line, burden of family, children, payment of debt due to expenditure occurred during attending inquiry and investigation of the case and overall the matter of livelihood and survival.

Table-4: Nature of Torture Victimization in Police Custody

Nature of Torture Victimization		Number	Percent (%)
Nature of arrest	Arrest with warrant	4	25%
	Arrest without warrant	12	75 %
	Total	16	100.0 %
Crimes of Arrest	Petty Crime	4	25.0 %
	Political Crime	9	56.3 %
	Murder	2	12.5 %
	Illegal Gambling	1	6.3 %
	Total	16	100.0 %
Number of taken to the custody	First time Accused	11	68.8 %
	Second Time Accused	1	6.3 %
	Accused for Many Times	4	25.0 %
	Total	16	100.0 %
Stage of Torture	During Arrest and Pre-Trail	12	75.0 %
	Trail	2	12.5 %
	Sentencing	2	12.5 %
	Total	16	100.0 %
Reason of torture	Confession Obtain	8	50.0 %
	Receive Bribery	6	37.5 %
	Political Order/Organizational Order	2	12.5 %
	Total	16	100.0 %
Types of Torture	Physical Torture	10	62.5 %
	Psychological Torture	2	12.5 %
	Both Physical and Mental	4	25.0 %
	Total	16	100 %
Consequences of Torture	Physical Injury	11	69 %
	Mental harm	3	19 %
	Death	2	12.5 %
	Total	16	100 %

4.2.4 Cross-Tabulation analysis:

i) Comparison 1- Types of Crime in which Tortured Victim was Arrest * Nature of Arrest of Tortured victim

From cross table-1, among the total 16 incidents of police torture in custody, in case of petty crime 100 percent victim of police torture were arrested without warrant. Besides, in case of political crime, 11.1 percent victims of police torture were arrested with warrant and 88.9 percent victims of police torture were arrested without warrant. Also, in case of Murder and illegal gambling, 100 percent victims of police torture were arrested with warrant. So, during January to April, 2015 major victims of police torture were arrested without warrant under political crime which indicates the violent political situation.

Cross Table-1: Types of Crime in which Tortured Victim was Arrest * Nature of Arrest of Tortured victim

Types of Crime in which Tortured Victim was Arrest	Nature of arrest of Tortured victim				Total	
	Arrest with warrant		Arrest without Warrant			
	Number	%	Number	%	Number	%
Petty Crime	0	0 %	4	100 %	4	100 %
Political Crime	1	11.1 %	8	88.9 %	9	100 %
Murder	2	100 %	0	0 %	2	100 %
Illegal Gambling	1	100 %	0	0 %	1	100 %
Total	4	25 %	12	75 %	16	100 %

ii) **Comparision-2: Social Status of Victim* Number of Taken to the Custody**

From cross table-2, among the total 16 incidents of police torture in custody during January to April, 2015, 33 percent of victim of police torture in the police custody were poor and accused for first time. Besides, 66.7 percent of victim were poor and accused for many times. Moreover, 66.7 percent of victim of police torture in the police custody were lower middle and accused for first time while 16.7 percent of victim were accused for second times and 16.7 percent of victim were accused for many times by police. And, few percent of victim of police torture in the police custody were from middle class and upper middle class social status who accused for first time while same percent of victim were upper class background who accused for many times by police.

Cross Table-2: Social Status of Victim* Number of Taken to the Custody

Social Status of Victim	Number of taken to the custody						Total	
	First time Accused		Second Time Accused		Accused for Many Times			
	Number	%	Number	%	Number	%	Number	%
Poor	1	33.3 %	0	0 %	2	66.7 %	3	100 %
Lower Middle	4	66.7 %	1	16.7 %	1	16.7 %	6	100 %
Middle	5	100 %	0	0 %	0	0 %	5	100 %
Upper Middle	1	100 %	0	0 %	0	0 %	1	100 %
Upper	0	0 %	0	0 %	1	100 %	1	100 %
Total	**11**	**68.8 %**	**1**	**6.3 %**	**4**	**25.0 %**	**16**	**100 %**

ii) Comparison: 3- Types of Crime in which Victim was Arrest * Reason of Torture

From cross table-3, among the total 16 incidents of police torture in custody, in case of petty crime 100 percent victim of police torture were tortured to obtain confession. Besides, in case of political crime, 66.7 percent victims of police torture were tortured to obtain confession while 11.1 percent victims of police torture were tortured to receive bribery and tortured for political or organizational power. Also, in case of Murder and illegal gambling, 100 percent victims of police torture were tortured to obtain confession and bribery. So, during January to April, 2015 major victims of police torture were arrested under political crime who become the victim of police torture in the custody to obtain confession of unlawful offence by police.

Cross Table- 3: Types of Crime in which Tortured Victim was Arrest * Reason of Torture

Types of Crime in which Tortured Victim was Arrest	Reason of Torture						Total	
	Confession Obtain		Receive Bribery		Political Order/Organizational Order			
	Number	%	Number	%	Number	%	Number	%
Petty Crime	0	0 %	4	100 %	0	0 %	4	100 %
Political Crime	6	66.7%	1	11.1%	2	22.2 %	9	100 %
Murder	2	100 %	0	0%	0	0 %	2	100 %
Illegal Gambling	0	0%	1	100 %	0	0 %	100	0 %
Total	8	50 %	6	37.5 %	2	12.5 %	16	100 %

4.2.4 Hypothesis Testing

Hypothesis 1:

Null Hypothesis: Torture is not applied as a tool to extract confession in police custody.

Alternative Hypothesis: Torture is used as a tool to extract confession in police custody.

From Chi-Square table no 1, at 5% significance level and 6 degrees of freedom the tabulated value of chi-square is 12.59. But calculated value is 13.18. Calculated value is higher than table value with 5% level of significance in 6 degrees of freedom. According to the condition of hypothesis test the null hypothesis is rejected and the alternative hypothesis is accepted. In this situation it is mean that torture is used as a mechanism to extract confession in police custody.

Hypothesis Test Table 1: Calculated value

Chi-Square (χ^2) Test	Calculated Value	df	Significance level	Table value
Pearson Chi-Square	13.18	6	0.05	12.59

Hypothesis 2:

Null Hypothesis: Victims of torture in police custody are not belongs to young age from poor and middle class sections of society.

Alternative Hypothesis: Victims of torture in police custody belong to young age from poor and middle class sections of society.

From Chi-Square table-2, at 5% significance level and 16 degrees of freedom the tabulated value of chi-square is 24.99. But calculated value is 27.6. Here calculated value is higher than the table value with 5% level of significance in 16 degrees of freedom. According to the condition of hypothesis test the null hypothesis is rejected and the alternative hypothesis is accepted. In this situation it is mean that victims of torture in police custody belong to young age from poor and middle class sections of society.

Hypothesis Test Table 2: Calculated value

Chi-Square (χ^2) Test	Calculated Value	df	Significance level	Table value
Pearson Chi-Square	27.6	16	0.05	24.99

4.3 Thematic Analysis of KII Study

4.3.1 Drawbacks of Torture in Police Custody

The process of judicial investigation is not very much uncertain. Besides, the issue of investigation by police against police officers is not satisfactory as it has less public satisfactory. So, there is need to add another medium of investigation. There should be clear definition of custodial torture and death in the laws of Bangladesh like penal code. And using section 54, 164,167 of under this act is needed to be more specific. In case of punishment, both imprisonment and fine should introduce and imprisonment for life should be replaced by capital punishment in torture and custodial death prevention act.

Torture usually takes place during the initial stages of an arrest. If a lawyer contacts a victim after release from detention, there is a risk that visible signs of torture will have faded and that it will be more difficult to prove allegations of abuse. However, lawyers in our country seldom visit people in police custody (Rahman, 2009).

4.3.2 Upshot of Torture in Police Custody

The victim experience is passed to the family, community, social groups; impacts on feelings towards the police. Most of the victim of torture in police custody become physically incapable to move freely, suffering from severe pain in different parts of the body and even paralyzed, become fully depended on the medicine. All this facts are decreases their physical stability, looses mental stamina and socio-economic condition become very poor.

Solitary confinement can result in psychological trauma, including depression, anxiety, difficulties with concentration and memory, hypersensitivity to external stimuli, hallucinations and perceptual distortions, paranoia, suicidal thoughts and behavior, and problems with impulse control which causes significant cognitive impairments, including deficits in memory, learning, logical reasoning, complex verbal processing, and decision-making (Ojeda, 2008).

4.3.3 Initiatives for Assisting Victim of Torture in Custody

Police torture usually intended to hurt and humiliate, not to kill. It is a tactic used by the police to give the victim the guise of voice, and to displace the agency for the violence from the state to its subject at least in the governmental and judicial record. Victims of torture are not primarily interested in monetary compensation, but in having their dignity restored. Both public acknowledgment of the harm and humiliation caused and the establishment of the truth together with a public apology are critically important.

Justice is only perceived as such when criminal prosecution has lead to an appropriate punishment of the perpetrators. There is the need of long- term medical and psychological rehabilitation and activities that foster community support whether through traditional rituals or healing practices (Talal, 2010).

5. Conclusion

Custodial torture is prevailing in our society from the ages. Despite several initiatives in recent years, torture and ill treatment continues to be endemic throughout and continues to deny human dignity to thousands of individuals. Victimization of torture in police custody has become so common these days that not only the police and bureaucracy but even people take it for granted as a routine police practise of interrogation. Undoubtedly, the police are under a legal duty and have legitimate right to arrest and interrogate the offenders. In a democratic country like Bangladesh, it's the people and not the police who are the real masters as the sovereign power are rested with them. The police are simply the agent of the government which is ultimately accountable to the people.

However, in exercising this legal right police have to be aware that law does not permit the use of torture, cruel and inhuman treatment on an arrestee during the interrogation and investigation of an offence. It is certain that we want elimination of serious crime but arrest without warrant, remand in interrogation and custodial violence are not the solution. We need a strong and impartial guidance and commitment and combined effort of each and every one in the society as early as possible.

References:

Ain O Salish Kendra. (2014). *Strengthening Human Rights Defenders.* Retrieved at March 2, 2015 from http://www.annual-report-ask_14.pdf

Amnesty International. (2008). *Torture in the Eighties.* Amnesty International Publication Retrieved at January 25, 2015 from http://www.hrw.ahrc/asia/bangladesh

Asian Human Rights Watch. (2013). *Human Rights in Bangladesh,* Retrieved at January 30, 2015 from http://www.hrw.org/asia/bangladesh

Aziz, Adeeba. (2010). *Rights to freedom from torture.* Retrieved at January 6, 2015 from Rights to freedom from Torture.html

Bamford, D. & Sarre, R. (2000). *Factors Affecting Remand in Custody, in Research and Public Policy Series.* Canberra: Australian Institute of Criminology.

Basoglu, M. (2013). *Torture and its consequences: current treatment approaches.* Part IV. Cambridge University Press.

Berliner, P., Nikkelsen E.M., & Bovbjerg, A. (2004). *Psychotherapy treatment of torture survivors.* International Journal of Psychosocial Rehabilitation. Retrieved at April 8, 2015 from http://www.apt.ch/content/files_res/monitoring-police-custody_en.pdf

Catani, Claudia. (2013) .*The Tortured: In the Trauma of Psychological Torture,* Retrieved at April 8, 2015 from

http://www.univie.ac.at/bimtor/dateien/cambodia_omct_2003_police_torture.pdf

Hadi, Ashraful. (2012). *Freedom from Torture and Ill Treatment.* Retrieved at July 3, 2015 fromhttp://Torturous_law_enforcement_system_in_Bangladesh_Progress_Bangladesh.html

Halim, Abdul. (2009). *Text Book on Code of Criminal Procedure,* 3rd ed, Dhaka, CCB Foundation

Human Rights Watch. (2014). *Human Rights in Bangladesh,* Retrieved at April 28, 2015 from http://www.hrw.org/asia/bangladesh_2014

Islam, Soma. (2007). *Seeking Effective Remedies: Prevention of Arbitrary Arrest and Freedom from Torture and Custodial Violence.* Bangladesh Legal Aid and Services Trust, Dhaka.

Jafar Alam Chowdhary vs. State. 20 DLR 666

Jeevan, Reddy. (2001). *Custodial Crime: An Affront to Human Dignity and Human Right.* Universal Law Publication Pvt. Ltd., New Delhi, India

Khan, Hamiduddin. (2003). *Jurisprudence and Comparative Legal Theory*, Dhaka: Anupam

Gyan Bhandar prokasoni

Malik, Shadeen. (2007). *Arrest and Remand: Judicial Interpretation and Police Practice.* Bangladesh Journal of Law, Special Issue.

Munir, M. (1998). *Principles and Digest of the Law of Evidence (1872).* Retrieved March 9, 2015 from http://bdlaws.minlaw.gov.bd/print_sections_all.php?id=24

ODHIKAR. (2015). *Torture and ill-treatment in Bangladesh.* Retrieved at May 4, 2015 from http://odhikar.org/human-rights-monitoring-report-january-june-2015/

ODHIKAR. (2014). *Fact Finding of Torture.* Retrieved at May 5, 2015 from http://1dgy051vgyxh41o8cj16kk7s19f2.wpengine.netdnacdn.com/wpcontentuploads/2013/06/Fact-Finding-disappearance-Mahobbat-Kustia-2013-Eng.pdf

Ojeda, Almarendo E. (2008). *What Is Psychological Torture: In The Trauma of Psychological Torture.* Praeger press, Burlin.

Rafiqul, M & Solaiman, M. (2004). *Torture under Police Remand in Bangladesh: Culture of impunity forgross violation of human rights.* Asia-Pacific Journal on Human Rights and the Law. Vol. 4, Issue 2.

Rahman, Mizanur. (2009). *Torturous law-enforcement system in Bangladesh*. Retrieved at April 25, 2015 from Torturous http://www.law-enforcementsysteminBangladesh _ProgressBangladesh.html

Rana, Masud. (2013). *Rule of law and order situation in Bangladesh.* Retrieved at April 7, 2015 from http://Custodial Victim/Net/Ruleoflaw_LaworderSituationinBangladesh_ WIFIBD.html

Sikdar, Ansaruddin M. (2000). *The Code of Criminal Procedure (1898)*. Retrieved at April 8, 2015 from http://bdlaws.minlaw.gov.bd/pdf_part.php?id=75

Talal, Asad. (2010). *On Torture, or Cruel, Inhuman, and Degrading Treatment* in *New Delhi*. Oxford University Press.

The constitution of The Government of the People's Republic of Bangladesh. (1972). Retrieved at March 17, 2015 from http://bdlaws.minlaw.gov.bd/chapter.php?id=367

Torture and Custodial Death (Prevention) Act. (2013). Retrieved at March 3 28, 2015 from http://www.ilo.org/dyn/natlex/natlex4.detail?p_lang=en&p_isn=95798

United Nation. *(1984). Convention against Torture and Other Cruel, Inhuman or Degrading Treatment or Punishment.* Retrieved at April 28, 2015 from https://www.fas.org/sgp/crs/intel/RL32438.pdf.

United Nation. (1976). *International Covenant on Civil and Political Rights (ICCPR).* Retrieved at May 19, 2015 http://www.ohchr.org/Documents/Professionalinterest/ccpr.pdf

United Nation. *(1948). Universal Declaration of Human Rights (UDHR).* Retrieved at February 19, 2015 from http://www.un.org/en/universal-declaration-human-rights/

Appendix

Annexure 1: Loopholes of Different Legal Framework in Prohibition of Custodial Torture in Bangladesh

Bangladesh is obliged to incorporate the Convention against Torture and Other Cruel, Inhuman or Degrading Treatment or Punishment (5 October 1998) (CAT)'s rejection of torture. State parties to ensure that all acts of torture are offences under its criminal law (article 4(1). The same shall apply to commit torture and to an act by any person which constitutes complicity or participation in torture. Besides, any individual who alleges he has been subjected to torture in any territory under the jurisdiction has the right to complain and to have his case promptly and impartially examined by its competent authorities (article 13). Although our country has ratified this convention but these are not followed properly in the practice level.

Bangladesh is also bound to follow the International Covenant on Civil and Political Rights (ICCPR) also clarifies that no one shall be subjected to torture or to cruel, inhuman or degrading treatment or punishment entitles individuals to compensation for unlawful arrest or detention (article 7). But it is not properly followed in Bangladesh by law enforcers.

The Constitution of Bangladesh lays down fundamental principles of State policy, such as democracy and human rights (article 11). Article 27 establishes the right to equality before the law while article 31 provides for protection of law, and prohibits actions not taken in accordance with law. Besides, article 32 protects the right to life and personal liberty and Article 33 provides safeguards from arbitrary arrest and detention. Most importantly, article 35 provides explicitly that, No person shall be subjected to torture or to cruel, inhuman, or degrading punishment or treatment. Section 35(4) of the constitution states, no person accused of any offence shall be compelled to be a witness against himself. In addition, articles 44 and 102 of the constitution provide judicial remedy against any violation of fundamental rights. So the constitutional provisions are very clear against the torture, illegal detention before or after extracting confession. And according to section 35(5), no person shall be subjected to torture or to cruel, inhuman, or degrading punishment or treatment. But in spite of these keeping under custody beyond the period of twenty four hours and custodian tortures are very much regular affairs in Bangladesh.

According to the Penal Code (1898), conduct amounting to torture may be prosecuted under some specific offences like voluntarily causing hurt (Section 319 of) to extort confession or to compel restoration of property (punishable by up to seven years Imprisonment and liable to a fine (Section 330) and, if the hurt caused is grievous (Section 320 penal code), the maximum punishment is ten years imprisonment and liability to pay a fine (Section 321). So, there are many provisions to prevent any form of torture in our penal code and scope to ensure the rights of tortured victim. But few of this is followed in case of victim of torture in police custody in Bangladesh.

Notably, Section 167 of the Code of Criminal Procedure speaks about two types of custody- police custody and judicial custody. As per section 'police custody' can be granted for a maximum period of fifteen days only' Police custody basically means police remand for the purpose of interrogation. According to the Code of Criminal procedure, the requirements of law in recording a statement under section 164 of the code of criminal procedure read with section 364 of the same code are as follows. Firstly, the magistrate should give the accused presented before him sufficient time to think and contemplate. Secondly, The magistrate declares to the accused that he is a Magistrate not a police officer and also explains to him that he is not bound to confess and the confession may be used as evidence against him and he will not be returned to police custody if he will have confessed or not. Thirdly, the magistrate will record confession only when it appears to him that such confession is voluntary. Fourthly, the magistrate will ensure that there is no police personnel present in the room or within the sight or hearing of the accused. Besides, in cases of custodial deaths, an inquest, which is usually conducted by an executive magistrate, is mandatory (section 174 and 176 of CrPC) Where the police receive information indicating that a person has been killed by another or has died under circumstances raising a reasonable suspicion.

Regarding the investigation of the offences of custodial crime the Torture and Custodial Death (Prevention) Act, 2013, section 5(5) of the said the Court will direct a police officer not below the rank of the accused to investigate the offence. On the contrary, section 7(1) said that a third person can lodge a complaint of torture under this Act to a police officer not below the rank of the Superintendent of Police. Moreover, the Act does not specify the modus operandi of post mortem and the process of collecting post mortem report. If the investigation does not completed within the prescribe time limit, the Act does not provide any direction to what the procedure will be followed after that. Which types of offences will be treated as offence under this act is indicated in section 13. And section 14 clarified that the accused of tortured victim be punished with rigorous imprisonment of minimum life term or a monetary penalty of minimum one hundred thousand Taka or both, for that crime and in addition to that another compensation amounting to a minimum two hundred thousand taka must be paid to the victim/aggrieved person/persons. In spite of this entire legal guarantee, the citizens of Bangladesh persistently become the victim of the torture or cruel, inhuman or degrading punishment and treatment, especially in the custody of law enforcement agencies which demands to analyze the gaps and obstacles of implementing this act.

Annexure 2: Methods and Effects of Custodial Torture (Both Case Study and Content Analysis)

Victims of this study are shows that, physical injuries that result from torture may be classified as: minor and severe. Some physical injuries are visible, while others are not. It is not be possible to see all physical injuries but it is important not to assume that a victim is uninjured simply because there are no visible signs.

i. **Physical Torture Methods**
   a) Beating with rod, batons and bamboo whips;
   b) Kicked and slapped;
   c) Tied with rope;
   d) Threat of more severe torture.
   e) Squatting naked,
   f) Humiliation;
   g) Urinate pressure;
   h) Confined in dark cell,
   i) Hot water treatment;
   j) Cracking finger nails with pliers;
   k) Threat of killing;
   l) Hanging from the ceiling;
   m) Stripped naked

n) Inadequate food and water

o) Burn with cigarette;

p) Rolling;

q) Electric shock;

r) Red chili powder spread etc

ii)　Physical Torture Effects

a) Pain in several body parts;

b) Serious weakness;

c) Headaches and head trauma;

d) Fracture to bones;

e) Neurological Damage;

f) Skin damage and diseases;

g) Vision and hearing problems etc.

Psychological torture of this studies victim breaks down the human mind through a powerful assault on the victim's basic conditions for mental survival. Under normal circumstances, a victim responds to disruptions in homeostasis through periods of readjustment. The stress applied in torture, including psychological torture, is designed to elicit high levels of arousal without the appropriate action that allows arousal to readjust-

iii)　Psychological Torture Methods

a) Threatening to harm and kill to relatives

b) Forced witnessing or hearing the torture of others

c) Mock execution

d) Humiliations

e) Threat of cross-fire/ Goom killing to accused etc.

iv) Psychological Torture Effects

a) Re-experiencing the trauma

b) In appropriate or less emotions

c) Social withdrawal

d) Anxiety and depression

e) Panic disorder

f) Sleep disturbance

g) Fear and excess anger

h) Mistrust

i) Feeling of helplessness, isolation

j) Hypersensitivity

k) Disassociation and depersonalization

l) Thoughts of suicide etc.

Annexure 3: Required schemes to Prevent Torture in Police Custody in Bangladesh

When the police takes the liberty of an individual and places him or her in police custody; it assumes full responsibility for the protection of life and liberty of that person by state itself under the obligation of domestic and international human rights laws. Hence, following are some advice to prevent arbitrary arrest, torture and custodial violence, and reducing the victimization of torture-

i. Reduce the excessive and arbitrary arrest and torture;

ii. Ensuring accountability and advocacy of police;

iii.	Police should be free from political influence;
iv.	Establishing a monitoring cell to control abuse of police power;
v.	Ensuring fairness of justice process to combat police corruption;
vi.	Training and awareness on the human rights and victimization issue;
vii.	Motivational programmes and campaign for both police and victim of torture;
viii.	Ensuring the rights of torture victim through awareness, rehabilitation and compensation.

Copyright The Authors 2016

All liability with the authors

www.ingramcontent.com/pod-product-compliance
Lightning Source LLC
Chambersburg PA
CBHW070410190526
45169CB00003B/1199